AF486798

Title: Mother's Purpose ®
Author: Larissa Castro Jaén
(larissa.castro@padresactivos.com.ve) First Edition
Cover design, layout and illustration: Irene Castro
(irene.ccazes@gmail.com)
Printed in Lima, Peru
2019

Larissa Castro Jaén

Mother's Purpose

To my daughter Rebecca, who
has gifted me a new dimension
to the purpose of my life by
making me a mother.

Prologue

Have you ever wondered; Who am I? I am sure you have and I am also sure that your answer has been: I am the daughter of ..., or the wife of ..., or the mother of ...

None of them give the correct definition of who you are because first of all you are a woman and then, you play the other roles of your life, specially: that of mother. Motherhood is a difficult vocation to learn and there are no universities that prepares you for it, you learn and apply daily while you experience the corresponding successes and mistakes.

The author comes from a home where she is the 8th of 9 children, to which sons-in-law, daughters-in-law, grandchildren and great-grandchildren have been added. She has witnessed that the secret to the family unity, however large, is the practice of love in all its colors, appreciation, communication, empathy, listening, encouragement and respect.

From this line of thought it arises in her the concern to be trained with tools for encounters and communication in family homes, and in particular, led her to write Mother's Purpose which, more than a book, is a practical guide in which she has poured all her experience gathered in more than 10 years as a family advisor. Each page of the book has a reflection and its corresponding action note aimed to provide you the urge of creating a space of connection with yourself which allows you to take care of yourself and thus improve the relationship you have with your children. Putting into practice what is suggested in this book, will arouse a transformative action where love and respect for you and your children, will be present in the day to day to bring peace and harmony to your home.

Larissa Castro Jaén is Venezuelan, she lived for several years in Switzerland, then in Panama and now she currently resides in Peru. Since 2012 she is a certified instructor for Dr. Thomas Gordon's Effective and Technically Prepared Parent (P.E.T) courses. She desires to leave this work to her daughte Rebecca as a way to always be present in her life and with the aim for it to serve as a guide for her so she can be a mother with purpose when her time comes.

I am especially proud to write this foreword to my daughter's book, I am sure that with this book, she will achieve her commitment to help other mothers successfully take the helm of their homes without forgetting to value themselves as women.

Ligia Jaén de Castro

Introduction

Raising our kids, and the love we have for them, absorbs our attention with such intensity that we are able to forget our own needs as women. It is not a n isolated situation that, in some moment of our motherhood, we feel the need to recover, to rescue ourselves, to find ourselves again, to reach out for our desires, illusions and life projects.

In my ten years of experience as a family advisor, I have identified a main factor that directly influence the peace and harmony of a home. It is that daily moment of personal encounter that mothers set aside for themselves, which allows them to gain serenity and stability so that after they may be truly available in the upbringing of their children, therefor having the ability to connect emotionally with them and detect their requirements and necds. When the woman does not count with this "me" time, dissatisfaction, sadness, frustration or anger become frequent emotions that affect her and the rest of the family.

In each chapter of this book you will find 52 reflections with their respective action notes so that, during each week of the year, you may allow yourself to make time for a meeting with yourself, give a look at the parenting practices that you are applying with your children from your true self and also, that you may put into practice the activities that I suggest with the aim of gaining peace for yourself and for your home. Our role as a mother, if we live it consciously, will undoubtedly propel us towards personal growth. Through this book, Mother's Purpose, I will accompany you with each text so that you can make motherhood an excuse that will lead you to the beautiful encounter with yourself and to a deep and connected relationship with your children.

How to read Mother's Purpose?

- ⵛ You can start reading the book with the first chapter, in any week of the year.

- ⵛ If you like it, you can also read the chapters randomly or select that special text that catches your attention in the thematic index.

- ⵛ For a week, read the same chapter so you can internalize the topics and observe the benefits that putting the "action note" into practice will bring you.

- ⵛ Finally, you can also organize a group of friends and meet weekly to read the chapters in order to be nourished by the experiences of other mothers. The indications to start these groups will be found in the "annexes" session at the end of the book.

Index

Thematic Index

1
Everything has its moment

If everything has its moment and you agree with this sentence, why the desire to do so many things at once?

Your children will love you for one simple reason: you are their mother. They will love you for the sake of it, because you are their main source of love. Sometimes, as mothers we get exhausted by doing and doing a lot of things for them, thinking that by doing these actions it will make them love us more. It seems that, unconsciously, the affections that our children feel towards us, is generated as the result of the many actions we do for them. But this is not true, they will love us and we will be important in their lives because they have no other way to experience the child-mother relationship.

Action note:

Observe your eagerness and ask yourself How do I feel? Why do I always go on a race? What am I not delegating? What are the needs that I have as a woman and that I am not taking care of? Listen carefully to your answers, validate your emotions, and commit to treat yourself with kindness.

2

Do you consider yourself a mother in the best express style?

I n this world, where speed has come to possess a monumental value, we always live with our feet on the accelerator pedal in our mind, just as if we had to win a fictional race against our own requirements and the other's as well. No wonder, at the end of the day, we feel exhausted and with the feeling of not having done enough. Does this happen to you?

Action note:

When you wake up, and before you get out of bed, breathe several times, become aware of being alive, thank God for everything you have around you, allow yourself to be in the present moment and then start your activities. With this little exercise, your mind will be more focused and you will gain peace of mind.

3
I love you just because

My child, having you has been a blessing, because of this I deeply appreciate your life and accept you as you are.

I understand that you did not come into the world for me, nor because I needed it. I may have been deluded into believing that part of what was your responsibility was to meet my expectations. Actually, you don't need to "be" something I want, because you already "are", you are complete. You came into this world with a soul that seeks to express itself and I feel honored to be, that other being, who is willing to accompany you and guide you in this mission. I understand that your worth is intrinsic to your existence and, in the expression of your humanity, you are sufficient.

Action note:

When your child is in a quiet moment, embrace them serenely, let them feel the peace of mutual affection and, as you give them a kiss, tell them "I love you just because".

4
Feel

There are propitious days to feel and grant
us to experience an emotion. When we
connect with our feelings we access that
personal space that serves as an encounter
with the being that we are and that shows us
the route to peace.

Action note:

This week, try to take three breaks during
the day. These moments can be performed
in the morning, in the afternoon and before
bedtime. Take four deep breaths in each of
your breaks, and identify how you feel in that
moment. Don't dwell on the rational motives
that justify your emotion, just let yourself be
felt, see how the emotion is reflected in your
body, accept it and let it go.

5

We don't need to confirm outside what we already know inside us

Whether your child has come through you or for the greatness and expansion of your heart, you are a mother and inside you are all the answers you are looking for about raising your children.

If you manage to turn down the volume to external comments and turn up the volume to what you are feeling in each situation, you will be able to find your beliefs, your reason and your intuition. Tune in to your mother's instinct, give yourself a vote of confidence because the relationship with your child is bidirectional but also unique, it's only between you and them.

Action note:

Observe those thoughts of doubts you have about raising your children, identify the emotions that generate you, write down what worries you and the feeling you have about it. Then take a breath and say out loud "in me is the answer and I trust". From the certainty that within you is the wisdom that will guide you towards the right solutions, you will begin to see clearly the ideal alternatives for you and your child.

6
Before mother, woman

Today the meeting is with you. Being a mother has only been an adjoining experience to your beautiful life, your children have only given you the opportunity to expand the experience as a woman that you already are.

That's why it's important that you devote time and attention to the main source from which the mother came, yes, you as an individual person, as the woman you are. If you stick only to your maternal role and do not attend to your needs as a woman, you will depersonalize little by little and, as a result, you will cease to be who you are, creating over time a void within you. You do not have to wait for the children to leave home to feel that emptiness, you can take care of yourself from now on and decide to nourish your life as a woman.

Action note:

Do you remember those songs that you have always liked and that cause you an automatic joy? How long have you been waiting to read that book or meet that friend for coffee? Don't wait any longer! Take action and give your children a happy, serene, stable mother who teaches them to love themselves by observing how you meet your own needs.

7
How much to thank!

It doesn't matter if you're going through a difficult time, if you look around, there's a lot to be thankful for.

You can decide to thank God for the sight, for breathing, for understanding what you read, for life, etc. Even in the hardest moments, you always have this opportunity to focus on how much you have to be thankful for. The benefit of opting for this attitude changes the focus, making it easier for you to get out of drama, get rid of complaints and stop the suffering.

Action note:

Look at everything you have around you, starting with your children, and look at those things you want to thank for and note them on a daily basis. Achieving a list with 200 sentences in a week, is a good exercise to modify your attitude towards life.

8
Love is implied by the senses

Yes, is that clear; in love there are two actors: the one who gives and the one who receives. However, in order for it to be experienced, it is necessary for this feeling to be seen, felt and heard.

It requires expressing love through our actions. The others cannot assume how much we love them and for this reason it will be necessary to demonstrate our affections through caresses, gestures and various acts of love.

Action note:

Think about how you think you give love to your family, and discuss with them if that's the best way to express it. Incorporate into your reflection those other ways in which you could also express yourself; perhaps you need more words, more actions, more caresses or attention.

9
The relationship

The relationship with a child is an indestructible link. If this is good, bad or regular, it is not a condition for the connection to be broken. This bond is never destroyed, there will always be a meaningful union between mother and child.

Now, if this relationship is so long-lasting and permanent, don't you think it's important to nurture it with the best ingredients?

Action note:

Look for information about what your children need according to their evolutionary stages so that you know what they need for their development; learn tools that allow you to identify what they think and how they feel according to their ages and what they require from you. By understanding their world more you will build a channel that, strengthened in love and respect, will transform for the better both of your lives.

10
What to choose for our mother-child relationship?

In your day to day and in this moment, you can decide to live in peace or without it. Peace is quietly within us and flees whenever there are shouts, comparisons, ironies, punishing silences, indifference, desire to always be right, strong arguments, distressing thoughts in the future, or sad thoughts of the past.

In the midst of these scenarios it is advisable to breathe as a first action, after "realizing" some of these behaviors. On a preventive approach, we can also consciously incorporate actions that promote serenity in our lives and in that of ours.

Action note:

Identify the factors that alter your mood so that you can take care of them; maybe they have to do with your unmet needs, with the situation you're in at a certain moment, or related to the behavior of your children. Also observe those actions that fill you and your family with peace, and begin to choose them. Living in peace is a right of every human being and you deserve it.

11

How do you want your child to remember you?

There is a journey that we can make at this precise time, it will allow us to become aware and even direct our actions of the day with sense and congruence. It is the one that begins in the future, asking ourselves How do I want my children to remember me? ; and then visualize us returning to the present moment.

When we allow ourselves this reflection, we can identify the kind of relationships we want to have with our children and see if the actions we take today are congruent with the affections and behaviors we long to have from them in the future.

Action note:

Respond and write on your diary or on a paper you may have at constant sight, how you want your child to remember you, and keep it in mind so that that intention floods your words and actions today.

12
The mother's friends

Motherhood embraces a space of emotional and mental time of such magnitude that some activities and people are automatically left out of our daily lives. One of these elements is the mother's friends.

However, an effort needs to be made to bring them back again, for women need to be constantly heard because it is a natural way, we have to drain our intense emotions. We also need help and support from other mothers to give us containment and make us feel that we are not alone in this sometimes-exhausting role.

It is essential to make spaces to express that woman we are and that exists long before we have incorporated into our lives to be wives or mothers.

Action note:

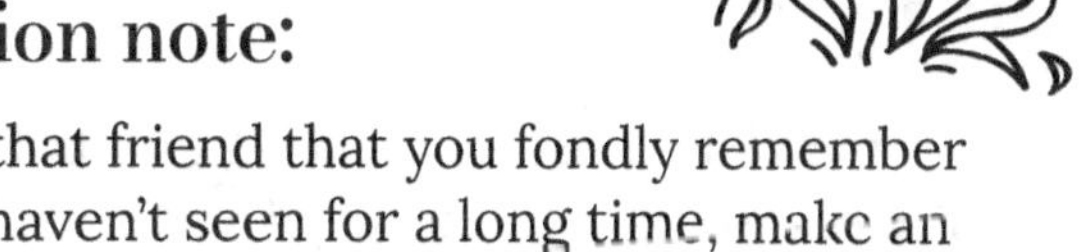

Call that friend that you fondly remember and haven't seen for a long time, make an appointment and meet her for a conversation.

Remember that a relaxed woman who attends to her needs will be a mother with more possibility of being available, mentally and emotionally for her children.

13
Maternal frustration

Without hesitation, frustration is one of the feelings we mothers' experiences more often. We live in a continuous, creative and loving effort for our children to achieve what they have, and what they most do: study, eat, bathe, pick up, talk to their grandparents, to order, brush their teeth, homework, etc.

Any other day, and more often than we would desire, frustration knocks on our door and enters our live without permission, overwhelming us with thoughts like: Things are never the way I organized them! Why can't I move forward and I'm always stuck in the same place? I no longer know how to make my child change his/her behavior, etc.

In order to return to our Inner balance, frustration needs to get out of our body first. To deny it and thinking "everything is under control" is to harvest an emotionally explosive reaction in the future.

Action note:

It is functional to look at frustration, recognize it and accept it. Express it through various techniques that will help you overcome and better accept your situation; such as writing a letter describing how you feel, isolate yourself in the bathroom to unburden, going for a run while clarifying your thoughts; etc. I must say as a suggestion do not practice violence as a steam reliever method, neither for you nor for others.

14
The eyes are the window of the soul

This is a saying that comes from ancient times and expresses that, through the gaze, we can see beyond the physical appearance to observe the being or the soul of whom we look.

Action note:

Have you looked your children in the eye today? And your partner? Looking into the eyes is a task that we leave aside because of the routine, but it is the first step to meet and connect with the other, it is the best way to start being present.

15
Sorry for the inconvenience, mother under construction

Only with death do mothers stop building ourselves. While we live, there will always be an opportunity to learn and improve ourselves. Like children, we do not have a manual, each experience is valid and gives us a space to advance to the next level of personal growth.

Action note:

Today you can decide to strip yourself of perfection and look at yourself with kindness from love. Today you can appreciate what the role of mother has made you grow as a woman, realize the blessings you have in life and begin to thank. Today is a perfect day to accept you and give you permission to love yourself.

16
The base feeling

There are pleasant emotions and others that are unpleasant; both come from previous thoughts that end up becoming feelings.

From motherhood and often unconsciously, we raise and educate children based on an emotion that can be positive or negative for their development.

For example: when a child falls, my reactions may be conditioned by a previous feeling of fear or confidence; to this fact, my responses as a mother will be based on my experiences. True?

Action note:

Pay attention to the emotions that are generated from your children's behaviors. Explore your feelings, look deeper and see if the basis of your reactions has to do with fear or confidence. The base feeling that you discover in yourself, will be the guide to start your own transformation, as a woman and as a mother.

17
The next level

Love is not a feeling, it is a decision. This is
so true that a mother may be tired, irritated,
hurt or feeling devalued and, however, she
is able to rise above all those current feeling
and go higher to decide to make an act of love
for your child.

This act of utmost goodness comes from the
soul. It is experienced in times of difficulty or
pressure and is able to transform us to reach
the next level of greatness as human beings.

Action note:

Just watch out for the moments when
you can decide to go above and beyond to
diminish your egos and join in action to your
own greatness, going to the next level of love

18
Being a mother is an excuse

God, in His infinite imagination, has made us a beautiful being with the ability to breed our children in the womb, or to majestically expand our hearts to adopt a child from the deepest love.

In the end, it seems that everything is an excuse to make motherhood the protective nest, the refuge from anguish, the warm and safe arms where a child always wants to come back, the soft wings that welcome a child, the attentive glance and the eyes ready to satisfy their needs, the whisper that lulls them, the song that is remembered until elderly years and the love that is palpable.

Action note:

Enjoy watching God use you to expand His love through you, from Him come all your beautiful acts and your motherhood is just an excuse for love. Trust that He is in charge.

19
Let grow

We have been created by Love to love. When we become mothers, we begin to experience a different love, the one we know it grows in us every day, becoming bigger continuously and infinitely.

This sublime experience clings us to our children in such a way that we won't want them to grow up or leave our side one day. It is in these thoughts that we nest fear in our minds and we lend ourselves to minimize or invalidate the potentialities of our children, thereby depriving them of the opportunity for them to build their own independence, autonomy and freedom.

Action note:

Think about those things you do that your children already have the capacity to do, teach them how to do them or explain to them how important certain values are to you, but then let them go and let them experience them without your eyes or your words being on them.

20
The Hidden Need

Every time we don't validate a need of our children, we're practicing a type of violence. Behind every tantrum, stew, face of supplication, anger or what we can describe as manipulation, there is a valid need that is hidden behind the initial expression.

It is likely that our children are asking for appreciation, attention, affection, security, listening, closeness or love; and each of these needs are valid and important for the healthy development of the human being.

You may not accept the way they express what they require for their lives, but it is our responsibility as an adult to identify what they want to tell us so that we can validate and address their needs.

Action note:

Faced with the cases described in the first paragraph, breathe and think that it is not about you but about them, that it is your children who are experiencing intense emotion and need your help. Look beyond the external behavior, reflect the emotion you see in them and be attentive to identify the need behind the initial expression.

21
Inherited behaviors

Our brain is designed to automatically and unconsciously repeat all those behaviors and expressions that have been learned throughout our lives, especially those assimilated during the first seven years of age.

No wonder, we are suddenly surprised by the awareness that we are repeating to our children, just those phrases and gestures that mom or dad had with us Does these happens to you? We end up transmitting what we have inherited.

Action note:

Identify and write down those expressions or gestures that you are repeating unconsciously and that you do not want to continue leaving in inheritance for the next generations. All behavior that is expressed unconsciously, begins to change when we make them conscious, because only from that space can we initiate real actions of transformation.

22
Notion of time

At around 9 years of age, children do not have a clear notion of time. This brings as a consequence that every time we give them an order, they assume that they can perform it now, later, tomorrow, or when they finish playing. They have no idea what 5 or 10 minutes are, nor do they know exactly what you mean when you say "in an hour you have to be ready to go out."

Action note:

Every time you give your child an order, add the adjective of time in a way that is understandable for them, for example: "go for a bath, now", "as soon as that little thing is over, you turn off the tv", "immediately, pick up the toys", "I'm going to be on a trip, but it will be done after night and day repeats twice, then mom will be with you again."

23
"Tips" for mothers

Given the stressful rhythms in which we live, where time seems to be running and pass you by, we also feel that parenting requires going at an accelerated pace. We nest the illusion that we can exercise motherhood and be effective in parenting just as quickly through "tips" that change the behaviors of children or teach us to be "better" mother.

However, parenting is a process, a long road that must be traveled, a path where step by step your children are growing and you are becoming a mother. We are product of the encounter, of the construction serene and in the present, of nourished conversations, of daily examples, of many hugs and of significant connection with the other; bottom line, we are human and we require time to form ourselves.

Action note:

Set aside today 10 minutes to share with your child alone, create a one-on-one encounter, find a space in the day to play with him or her, without any electronic device, look at your child in the eye and tell him or her that this time is only for him or her and that you will both have it every day. You will be opening the door for encounter, communication, trust and love.

24
Power

There is no dispute that parents have power over children because, without us, our little ones put their lives at risk. They need us to survive and this dependence places parents on a level of real and tangible power over them.

The difficulty with power is when we use it to impose solutions to conflicts with children. The moments in which we use force, impose ourselves, manipulate, reward, punish and forget to see and validate the needs that our children have behind their behaviors, are accurate samples of the exercise of a power that promotes resentment and puts at risk the relationships with the children.

Action note:

When you have a problem with your child, instead of using power in some of its forms, try to open a communication space so that you can identify their needs and that they also understand yours. From that mutual understanding, they can then explore possible solutions to the problem that are valid for both of them, and where both achicve the satisfaction of their needs.

25
A balm of peace

Mothers are not perfect. On a daily basis we find ourselves carrying out inappropriate actions of which, more sooner or later, we regret immediately pulling out the whip of guilt to reproach us for how "bad mother" we are.

If we believe ourselves to be perfect, we fail; if we think we are human, we get it right. It is beneficial for you and your children to recognize that you make mistakes and take this opportunity to enrich your relationship with them through healing words like: sorry, you're right, or excuse me.

Action note:

Put away the whip of guilt and pull out the balm of forgiveness. If you identify any inappropriate action that harms or offends your children or your partner, do not hesitate to try to ask for forgiveness and regain your and your love one's peace.

26
A magic rule

Harmony at home is a condition longed for by all, and especially mothers, we work hard so that everyone at home feels good.

I give you a rule that is learned in the course of " Parent Effectiveness Training "P.E.T. of the Dr. Thomas Gordon and it's really magical to achieve this goal.

Action note:

It consists of attending 3 family moments and investing daily quality time in each of them.

1.-Family time: it is the one in which everyone shares an activity (cooking, playing, accommodating the house, etc.).

2.- Time one by one: it is to spend 10 minutes with each member of the family, in an individual meeting and it is necessary to say that this activity will be daily.

3.- Alone time: this will be the space for you, where you can do what you like, where you can be with you, with your thoughts, your emotions and your illusions. If you can open a place for each of these points, you will be acting congruently towards harmony in your home.

27
Smoke signals

All our behaviors reflect a message. With every word or gesture we are transmitting information that, consciously or not, seeks to be communicated. Thus, for example, children make gestures or tell us words that denote a hidden need for it to be validated and attended to by us.

Action note:

Connect with your child's need whenever he or she makes "smoke signals" to get your attention. It may be that your child's way of communication is through crying, complaining, restlessness, bad mood or silence. Observe and help, because you are the right person to support your child.

28
The one that does everything

The anxiety produced by exhausting routines of action often hides the need to feel. loved by others. The perennial "robotic" doing that solves the lives of others is an inappropriate way that some mothers use to tell their own "I love you, and please don't stop loving me."

When our relationships are based on the feeling of anxiety about being loved, we fall into harmful behaviors both to us and to those around us.

Action note:

Identify those actions that you "do" and that you feel you cannot stop doing them because they cause you a lot of concern. Ask yourself if it is possible to delegate them, not if others are able to do them, but rather if you can let go of them, if the answer is "yes", take the step and hand the action to others. Recognize in front of yourself and others that you also need rest and you also need to feel loved for who you are and not for what you do.

29
An important network

When we become mothers, we seem to fall into a deep pit, so absorbing and full of love that we forget our needs; including those to be heard and understood.

It is important to understand that an endless number of mothers are experiencing this same situation, and probably at the same time; feeling alone, isolated and with many doubts about their role.

Perhaps all we need is to be able to express that we require help, to be heard in order to identify each other, and to open the door to a real and immense community of women who feel and own the same urgencies.

Action note:

Look for those mothers and friends with whom you feel identified, heard and respected. Value and take care of them as an indispensable element for your life, because they are part of that important network that adds value, helping you to drain and feel supported.

30
Congruence

It's a logical relation that spins together what I think, what I do and what I say. Congruence can be considered as one of the most challenging values we can choose in life, and that seems to never finish to grow in us because, as we incorporate knowledge into our minds, we adjust it to the daily work and what we express.

Some phrases such as: "I hit you because I love you", "if you wanted me, you would do what I tell you", "I suffer for love", shouting at the child "do not yell at me" or, as soon as they fall, tell them "stand up that nothing has happened".

Action note:

Listen and observe what you think, say and do. Seek to connect these three actions in your life consciously and you will experience the tranquility of congruence.

31
Everything passes

That's right, and you can read it again: "everything passes"; the good, the bad and the regular. There is no situation that is static or that lasts for a long time in our lives. Just as the water flows from the river into the sea, so our circumstances end up changing or drive us to transform ourselves.

We can choose to worry, be distressed or take it as an opportunity to learn, to strengthen ourselves or perhaps to enjoy the moment and be grateful. How you see situations pass in your life is a personal choice, the view and interpretation you give it, only has your stamp.

Action note:

Use every opportunity to look at you, to listen to your inner voice and allow yourself to decide how you want to live your process of becoming a mother. Enjoy the existence of your children and start your day by thanking your blessings.

32
The natural

We naturalize what becomes constant. Everything that is repeated becomes the norm, the common and the natural. It is what happens with all those actions that are born of fear and are expressed with violence; but it also happens with those who sprout from love and express peace.

Custom makes most of our behaviors "normal." Motherhood is a great opportunity to pass through the filter of consciousness all those beliefs that have shaped our behaviors throughout life. The benefit of this is to get out of "automatic mode," and start choosing what we want for our children, for ourselves, and for our families.

Action note:

Answering any of these questions can provide some light on your free will: How do I want to experience my motherhood? How do I feel about this behavior I have toward my children? What I'm doing arise from fear or love? What do I want the atmosphere in my home to be like? Am I taking consistent steps to achieve this?

33
The transforming force

Love is the greatest transforming force that exist. There is no energy in the world that generates more change than this, and it comes from an inexhaustible source: God.

Whenever your actions are infused with love, the Creator lives in you and expresses himself to your beloved ones.

To say words like I love you, I am sorry, thank you, I need you, you are important to me, I respect you, I value your life and your existence, etc., is to express sounds of affection that transform our lives and those around us. Gestures full of hugs, caring looks, talking kindly, doing a favor or hugging, make love become an experience.

Action note:

Put into practice what transforms and elevates you, return to love, and bring God into your life and family.

34
The Magic of Forgiveness

Only those who ask for forgiveness teach to forgive. It is a courageously liberating act and, whoever experiences it, enjoys peace and healing. Every mother, as a human being, is assured of error in her actions and from this reality she enjoys two fundamental rights: the right to "screw up", and the right to "fix it". The first corresponds to our human essence, and the second to the greatness of our soul. A mother who knows how to apologize for her mistakes teaches her children that there is a level that is above all role where both love and respect each other.

Action note:

When you want to apologize to your child, look for a time when you're both at peace, start by saying how you've felt about your behavior, strive to find a more descriptive feeling that isn't just, "I feel bad," and then ask for forgiveness.

35
When empathy is most needed

When your child doesn't obey you, or is experiencing a strong, uncontrolled emotion, or just doesn't listen to what you tell them; you'll likely start to feel despair, fear of not knowing how to handle the situation, or fear of losing control over your child. At that moment your intense emotions hijack your reason limiting your ability to be empathic with your child. In the moment in which your child has a problem and therefore expresses a strong emotion, is when he most urges a mother who can be present and emotionally available, who can help him manage his emotions.

Action note:

When this is the case, these three steps will help you:

.- Breathe. If you take a deep breath, about twice, you'll be able to stay in the present and get out of your personal bubble.

.- Validate your child's emotion. He recognizes that it is he who is having a problem and needs your help, which by the way, is the best in the world.

.- Be prepared to listen with empathy. Discover from your heart why your child is experiencing that emotion and let your child know. He or she will then tell you if he or she is feeling understood or not.

36
On another level

Being a mother is the opportunity to live a spiritual state on another level that undoubtedly transforms the existence. It is an excuse to experience unconditional love, to rise up to feel goodness and to expand this nobility of feeling toward others, including all other children.

It is a divine gift that leads us to the sublime connection with another being.

> "When you have a child, you have all the children of the earth"
> Andrés Eloy Blanco

Action note:

Observe yourself beyond your actions, look at yourself from the emotion of your dedication, elevate yourself in kindness and joyfully enjoy the blessing of this experience of being a mother.

37
Power relations

A power relationship results when, in the face of the need of the other, I impose my solution or, in the face of my need, you impose yours. From these two educational styles are generated: authoritarian and permissive. Educating from these positions turns family relationships into nests of conflict and unmet needs. They are called "win-lose" relationships because there is one who claims to win by imposing his solution on the other who feels he/she has lost.

On the other hand, when both sides talk about their needs and validate each other, they solve their problems and come out of them stronger. This is the principle of a respectful and democratic relationship.

Action note:

A conflict in the family can be successfully resolved if each party expresses its need and among all validates them. Only from there can we seek common solutions that allow household members to meet their needs, be happy and emerge victorious from the problem. This is called a "win-win" conflict resolution.

38
What kind of label qualifies you?

What label would you use after "I'm a mother…"?

The word that comes at the end of that sentence may be becoming a label that seeks to describe a part of you, an emotion, a situation, or a behavior. When you label your motherhood, you simplify it, box it in and reduce it to its minimum expression. You are much more than impatient, strict, loving, consenting, permissive, authoritarian, single, etc. Your motherhood goes far beyond your emotions, your educational style, your ideas, your behaviors and, of course, has nothing to do with your marital status.

Your motherhood is a human experience that encompasses everything you feel, do, think, experience and say.

Action note:

Describe your experience from your behaviors or actions. This will help you not to label yourself, thus avoiding minimizing the greatness of your motherhood; for example: "right now I feel with little patience" (Vs. I'm impatient), "I enjoy giving kisses and hugs (Vs. I'm loving), "I've decided to raise without my partner" (Vs. I'm a single mom).

39
A lot of distance

If your children are young, you may notice that there is a lot of distance between the level where your eyes are and theirs.

Put yourself in their place for a moment and imagine that in order to talk to someone you have to turn your head towards the sky and thus be able to look at the eyes of the other. From that great distance would you feel close to that person? This is how your little ones may feel, distant from you, with a lack of encounter, distant from heart.

Action note:

When your child is experiencing intense emotion, whether pleasant or unpleasant, lower to their level, make proper eye contact, and make it easy to meet. This is the first step in welcoming and making ourselves available when they need us.

40
When impatience wins us

Do you certainly have days when you feel like you can't do it anymore and you're going to end up exploding with screams, crying, punishing your children heavily or getting sick? Well, yes, it happens to all of us, you're not alone in this.

And not taking time to identify, recognize and validate those factors that lead you to feel pressured. is what makes despair, frustration and helplessness grow in you.

Action note:

Acknowledge what were the facts that made you lose your patience. Sometimes in motherhood these factors are related to insisting on being right, maintaining control, having high expectations, doing many things at once, not sleeping well, some condition or evolutionary stage of your child that surpasses you, or perhaps it is the place where you are and in the conditions in which you live. Identifying is the first step so you can move on to the second: validate your emotions and seek help. Don't neglect yourself, mommy! You are the calm center where your children rest.

41
The love that transforms

The people whom you really have a power of influence are very close to you: you and your family. That's why, whatever you want for society, for politicians, for your neighborhood or your country, you can change it from your nearest area; that is, from your life and in your home.

"If you want to change the world, go to you home and love your family

Madre Teresa de Calcut

Action note:

If you want a different society, look within yourself and in your family, answering these questions with the aim of looking at the congruence and the area of action to attend to: do I live this in my life? Am I an example o this to my family? Do I take care of everyone in my home to live and experience that value

42
Today's children

Today's children need to have mothers from today and not from the last century. It is necessary to educate children with skills to function in a current society and not for one that no longer exists.

The problem is that it is a challenge to update ourselves in a world that is advancing rapidly in terms of technology, digital communication and social references.

Action note:

There is no safer and more permanent basis over time than educating children in values, because everything else is trendy and fades away. Make a list of your first five life values, write them down, and plan how to teach your children, with your own life model, those ideas and beliefs that have been useful and valuable in your life. With your example and congruence you can effectively influence the construction of values in your children and thus give them a safe path of action for the decisions they will have in their lives. They will choose whether to take your values or not, but you will have made your best delivery.

43
Your children, my children

One possible scenario is that your children will live in the same world as my daughter, and that means that they will share a tomorrow that we don't know. There is no way to know if they will find each other, meet or connect; however, they will inhabit a world with the same realities and challenges that they will have to attend to and face.

Action note:

If you educate yourself in parenting, grow as a person, and awaken awareness, you will directly influence your children's future; and the more mothers we motivate ourselves to do so, the better the world they will live in. I appreciate the effort you make to sow a better humanity for your children and for my daughter.

44
Influencing their lives

Always, forever and ever, parents will be influencing the lives of children. Throughout their existence, we will hover daily in their minds, feelings and actions. It is not an option for us, it is a tacit power that nature has given us and, through which, we deposit in them a series of sayings, beliefs, emotions, behaviors, phrases, experiences, looks, gestures, etc.

For this reason, it should not be an alternative to choose to form ourselves as mothers, since our children from their innocence, they believe in everything from us, they expect everything and trust everything.

Action note:

We are building our children's lives; that is why it is important that you look for information about parenting, you train through courses for parents, you let yourself be advised and accompanied by professionals who help you travel this beautiful path where you become a mother while building the life of your children.

45
The human dimension we forget in parenting

We mothers are looking forward to raising and educating our children in all its dimensions: the physical, the intellectual, the relational and the emotional; but what about the spiritual dimension?

To neglect to educate them for eternity, for the soul, for the permanent, is to leave in them a need without attend, impelling them to satisfy it through other elements that could be more harmful, such as excessive materiality, social status, food, the superficial, drugs, alcohol, etc.

Action note:

The soul is a spiritual dimension that needs the nourishment of love, transcendence and the eternal. Gain peace and silence, pay attention and listen to yours, and then lead your children by example. Don't neglect it because it gives meaning to human existence

46
No Interruption

One of the stressors that mothers have is the inability to perform tasks in the home without being interrupted; as a consequence, we need to rethink What was I doing? What did I come to look for? Where was I going? These constant pauses result in a waste of time that affects the performance of the tasks that we have planned for the day.

Action note:

To make a list the night before of the pending things to do and mark which ones you consider to be the priority, will allow you to be focused on the next morning and move forward effectively in the tasks you want to achieve.

47
The unpredictable

There are times in motherhood when parenting becomes completely unpredictable; we do not know what is happening, what is going to happen, what our children need and, above all, how we will solve the unforeseen.

If these situations become very frequent we can fall into high stress states that can compromise our health.

Action note:

In the face of the unpredictable, try, first of all, to gain mental serenity and decide to turn down the volume of toxic and repetitive thoughts. Take a deep breath, focus on the act of breathing, identify the emotion you feel and observe how it expresses itself in your body. Stay in the present and look at yourself, trust and give the situation to God, while you take the necessary steps to advance in the solution.

48
The Myth of Maternal Perfection

The paradigm of the perfect mother, the one who behaves peacefully and self-controlled, it is an unrealizable fantasy. It is impossible to stay that way permanently; however, it seems that we have mythologized motherhood and that "flawless" behavior is expected from us. This is so engraved in our behavioral patterns that even we ourselves find ourselves aspiring to this "heroic greatness" of the perfect mother that exists only in the collective imagination.

Action note:

When you feel any unpleasant emotion, let it be pain, sadness, helplessness, exhaustion, frustration, etc., express that feeling in words to your family members, tell them why you have that emotion and the behavior you require from them in order to alleviate your feeling. You will be able to drain the intensity of your emotion and at the same time, they will understand you.

49
Parenting?... for tomorrow

Just as we are trained to have a profession in life and in it we invest time, focus, money and effort; it is necessary that we assume that to raise from consciousness, we need to learn, form and act from knowledge. It must be a priority in life that our children have a meaningful and healthy existence, far beyond an excellent education; and this is built from parenting. It is through the relationship with the children where we manage to infuse an identity full of self-value, security, acceptance, appreciation for life, sense of belonging, nourishment for the soul and the experience of joy to exist.

Action note:

You are the mayor influence for your children, don't leave it in the hands of others. Taking this as a starting point, look for information and trust yourself, invest time, effort, money and focus so that you educate your children from consciousness and not by chance. You may not be present, but their tomorrow will thank you.

50
The perfect children

Yes, the perfect children... those that do not exist neither in your house, nor in mine.

It is healthy, both for our children and for us, to accept and enjoy the unique and unrepeatable particularity of each of our children.

Focus on their virtues and validate them. Use their "imperfections" to practice acceptance and tries to go above and beyond to detect the needs behind these behaviors.

Action note:

I give you what, every day, before I go to sleep and looking her in the eye, I say to my daughter: "I love you, I respect you and I value you."

51
Connecting spaces

Create spaces of emotional and relational
nutrition with your children and your partner.
Just as we have time for work or home affairs,
decide to take the time to play with your
children, thank them for their existence,
laugh as a family, dance with your partner,
pray together, see the stars, feel the breeze,
look into each other's eyes, etc.

Action note:

Without waiting any longer, today set aside
a meeting time for your loved ones and
experience the peace that the connection
with them gives you.

52
Look at Yourself

Never stop looking at yourself, but look at your life with kindness. Accept who you are and admit your greatness. You were already born with beauty, and motherhood has taken you to a higher level of beauty. Never minimize your needs and express yourself fluently. You are unique and unrepeatable and that is why the world expects your glow. God dwells in you and smiles of motherly love when you come to Him, trust His guidance, and make silence so you can hear Him.

Action note:

Every morning the day begins with you, with your essence. Pray before you start your morning and trust that God will accompany you and act on your behalf. Connect with your existence and love in action.

www.ingramcontent.com/pod-product-compliance
Lightning Source LLC
Chambersburg PA
CBHW081406130726
47998CB00011B/3094